How To Make Your Faith Work!

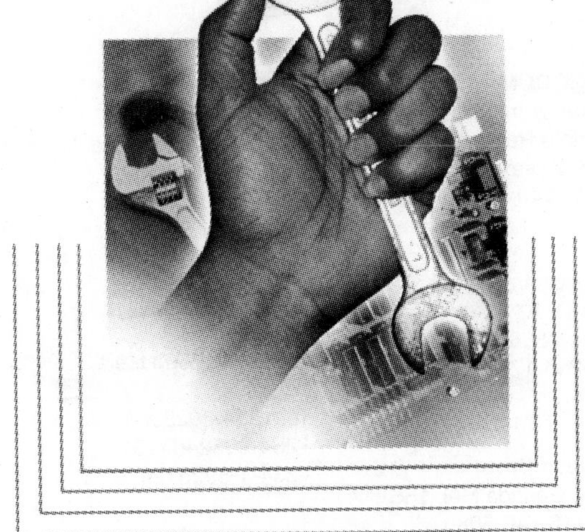

Chris Oyakhilome

How To Make Your Faith Work!
ISBN 978-37866-2-8

First Printing 2005, Second Printing 2007

All scripture quotations are taken from the *King James Version* of the Bible unless otherwise indicated.

BELIEVERS' LOVEWORLD INC.
aka Christ Embassy

UNITED KINGDOM:
Christ Embassy Int'l Office
363 Springfield Road
Chelmsford, Essex, CM2 6AW
Tel:+44 8451 240 440

USA:
Christ Embassy Int'l Office
2616 Texas Dr A,
Irving, Texas 75062
Tel:+1-972-255-1787

CANADA:
101 Ross Dean Drive,
Toronto, ON, Canada M9L 1S6
Tel/Fax:+1-416-746 5080

SOUTH AFRICA:
303 Pretoria Avenue
Cnr. Harley and Hendrik Verwoerd,
Randburg, Gauteng
South Africa.
Tel: + 27 11 3260038; +27 72760650
+27 767805242; +27 11 8863179

NIGERIA:
P.O. Box 13563 Ikeja,
Lagos.
Tel:+234-8023324188,
+234-8052464131,
+234-1-8925724

email: cec@christembassy.org
website: www.christembassy.org

Contents

Introduction

"I've confessed God's Word. I've sown seeds. I've fasted. I've prayed. I've done everything! Why hasn't my situation changed? Oh God, why?!!!" Many people are agonized like this over their seeming inability to change their situation. Yet, in Matthew 17:20, Jesus made this statement clear. He said "When you have faith as a grain of mustard seed, nothing shall be impossible unto you."

So, why do many of God's people pray, fast, cry,

sow seeds, confess Scriptures and still experience frustrations and even tragedies in their finances, health, jobs, marriages and businesses. Why do they always end up questioning, "Oh God, why?"

Many who find themselves asking this kind of question or who find themselves in such situations have one major problem: They haven't learnt how to make their faith work.

Apart from their ignorance of how to put their faith to work, some Christians find their faith coming under attack and weakened by adverse circumstances. Like Peter, they take their eyes off the Word and gaze in fear at the boisterous winds and billowing waves; they eventually begin to sink when they should actually be walking on the water.

Jesus said in the last days men's hearts shall fail them for fear (Luke 21:26), yet this is not the portion of the child of God. Proverbs 24:10 says, *"If thou faint in the day of adversity, thy strength is small."* **The Living Bible** translation of the same Scripture says,

"You are a poor specimen if you can't stand the pressure of adversity," letting us know it's wrong for our faith to fail or buckle under the pressure of adversity.

Unfortunately, it is at such times of adversity that some take their eyes off God's Word. They neglect their faith, allowing it to be stifled and rendered ineffective by circumstances which the same faith should have dominated. Any child of God can rise above any situation, time and time again, if he'd only learn how to make his faith work.

This book is the result of the urgent need by the Spirit of God to teach God's children how to make their faith work. I'll encourage you to make certain that you follow very carefully all the thoughts I share with you in this book.

You need to know how you can receive everything that rightfully belongs to you in Christ, and live the glorious, victorious, successful, joyous and prosperous life God has called you into.

Chapter One

The Faith To Live!

"Now faith is the substance of things hoped for, the evidence of things not seen. For by it the elders obtained a good report. Through faith we understand that the worlds were framed by the word of God, so that things which are seen were not made of things which do appear" (Hebrews 11:1-3).

It's very important that we have a clear understanding of what faith is before we proceed any further. In one of the most popular portions of scripture, faith is defined as the substance of things hoped for. If you have hope for anything, faith is what gives it substance. Faith gives you every reason to affirm something is yours before you see it with your physical eyes. Why? Faith is the substance of things hoped for; it calls real those things that are not physically observable. It calls them done NOW!

Faith is also defined as the evidence of things not seen, that is, the evidence of unseen realities. I do not see those things with my optical eyes but they're real to me. They're so real you can't take them away from me. Faith is the evidence of unseen realities. That means it is proof of the existence of something that is not tangible to the senses.

The Amplified Bible says,

> "...Faith is the assurance (the confirmation, the title deed) of the things [we] hope for, being the proof of things [we] do not see {and} the

> conviction of their reality [faith perceiving as real fact what is not revealed to the senses]"

Faith is the title-deed. If you bought a piece of land, you wouldn't carry the land with you everywhere, telling everybody, "See the land I bought." You would have documents to that land called "a title-deed." According to the Oxford English Dictionary, a title-deed is 'a document containing or constituting evidence of ownership.' If somebody requests for a proof of ownership, you can simply pull out your title-deed to the land and show them as proof of ownership. That's the evidence of unseen realities.

The land is real, but because you can't carry it around with you, they may not see it in your office. However, you have your proof of ownership – the title-deed; – something they can look at and say, "Yeah, you've really got that land."

Faith is not in the realm of the five physical

senses, since it is the proof of **things we do not see and perceive by our senses.** It also transcends the realm of reasoning and the mind. It's a spiritual force, an attribute of the human spirit. That's why I always like to define faith as the response of the human spirit to the Word of God.

Today's English Version of Hebrews 11:1 says, *"To have faith is to be sure of the things we hope for, to be certain of the things we cannot see."* Faith makes a certainty of things we don't see with our optical eyes. Therefore, faith is not an irrational leap in the dark but a leap on God's Word. It is believing what God's Word has said concerning anything and acting that way.

Now let me quickly point out here that there's a difference between faith and believing. Many people don't understand that difference.

Someone who's suffering from a form of sickness might cry, "Oh God, I believe! Oh God, I really know You can do it. Do it for me today! Heal me Lord!" He doesn't realize it but that's not faith. All he's doing is expressing his believing.

That fellow might be discouraged and unhappy if he doesn't receive healing, because he'll think to himself, "If I've ever had faith in my life, that was one time I had faith!" He'll be wondering, "Oh God, why didn't I receive?" not knowing that what he had was not faith at all.

Faith is the corresponding action to what you believe. I said earlier that faith is the response of the human spirit to the Word of God. For the one who is sick, when he hears the Word that says "By whose stripes ye were healed" and believes it, his response or corresponding action to that Word will be to begin to declare "By the stripes of Jesus, I was healed!" He should start acting as one who's been healed and as a result, begin to do the things he couldn't do hitherto, due to that sickness.

Now, when he declares that he is 'the healed' by the stripes of Jesus Christ, his declaration is not going to be based on his feelings, but on the Word of God that says he was healed.

James made reference to this aspect of faith when he said,

> "My friends, what good is it to say you have faith, when you don't do anything to show that you really do have faith? Can that kind of faith save you? If you know someone who doesn't have any clothes or food, you shouldn't just say, "I hope all goes well for you. I hope you will be warm and have plenty to eat." What good is it to say this, unless you do something to help? Faith that doesn't lead us to do good deeds

is all alone and dead!...Well, our ancestor Abraham pleased God by putting his son Isaac on the altar to sacrifice him. Now you see how Abraham's faith and deeds worked together. He proved that his faith was real by what he did. This is what the Scriptures mean by saying, "Abraham had faith in God, and God was pleased with him." That's how Abraham became God's friend. You can now see that we please God by what we do and not only by what we believe"

(James 2:14-17; 21-24) CEV.

For faith to be faith and not just believing, it's got to have some action to it. That's what James is telling us here. Your faith in God is demonstrated by your action.

You Can't Please God Without Faith

"BUT WITHOUT FAITH IT IS IMPOSSIBLE TO PLEASE HIM: for he that cometh to God must believe that he is, and that he is a rewarder of them that diligently seek him"

(Hebrews 11:6).

The Bible unequivocally states that *"without faith it is impossible to please him (God)."* It didn't say "without love" or "without prayer" or "without holiness;" neither did it say "without righteousness." I'm not saying these aren't important, for the Word of God lets us know they all are. What I'm saying is, it'll take faith to activate and appropriate these and many more blessings that are in the Word of God to your life.

Some have tried religiously all their lives to be

holy, to walk in love or to pray, yet they couldn't please God because they haven't learnt to walk by faith. It's impossible to walk in any of these successfully without faith. You're not expected to pray yourself into faith. How else would you be able to pray to the God you don't see? How do you know He's really up there listening to you? It's got to be by faith! So, you see, you do have faith. But now you have to learn how to make it work.

> "For I say, through the grace given unto me, to every man that is among you, not to think of himself more highly than he ought to think; but to think soberly, according as God hath dealt to every man the measure of faith"
>
> (Romans 12:3).

You believe the Bible is the Word of God and you study it, but you weren't there when it was written. You simply have faith that it's really God's

Word. That's where it all begins. Faith is fundamental; it's the foundation, for without faith you can't even be born again. It takes faith to come to God;

> "...for he that cometh to God must believe that he is and that he is a rewarder of them that diligently seek him"
>
> (Hebrews 11:6).

Hebrews 11:2 lets us know that *by faith the elders obtained a good report*. This is referring to men who have gone before us as examples, the patriarchs of faith such as Abraham, Isaac, Jacob, Moses, Samuel, David, Elijah and Elisha. The **Contemporary English Version** says, *"It was their faith that made our ancestors pleasing to God"* (**Hebrews 11:2).**

Hebrews 11 is popularly referred to as faith's hall of fame. It's a rich, inspiring and challenging catalogue of men and women who had fantastic testimonies of how they pleased God and did exploits in their generations because they walked by faith. They obtained a good report from God. He scored them highly for their faith, by the things they did and said, Hallelujah!

THE EXAMPLE OF NOAH

The Bible specifically exemplifies Noah as a man greatly blessed of God because he walked by faith in a generation that didn't acknowledge God. By his unwavering faith in God, he condemned the sinful world he dwelt in at the time.

One day, God looked upon the earth and was appalled at what He saw. The Bible says,

> "...God saw that the wickedness of man was great in the earth, and that every imagination of the thoughts of his heart was only evil continually. And it repented the Lord that he had made man on

> the earth, and it grieved him at his heart. And the Lord said, I will destroy man whom I have created from the face of the earth; both man, and beast, and the creeping thing, and the fowls of the air; for it repenteth me that I have made them. But Noah found grace in the eyes of the Lord"
>
> (Genesis 6:5-8).

God was ready to destroy the whole earth along with every last man and beast in it, but one man, Noah, found God's grace, because he was a man of faith. God told Noah He was going to destroy the world and gave him specific instructions on how to build an ark and select pairs of animals that will be preserved from the deluge. Being a man of faith, Noah followed all of God's instructions to the letter. No wonder the Bible says in **Hebrews 11:7** that he:

> "...being warned of God of things not seen as yet, moved with fear, prepared an ark to the saving of his house; by the which he condemned the world, and became heir of the righteousness which is by faith."

ABRAHAM: THE FATHER OF FAITH

Another great example of faith is Papa Abraham. God spoke to him one day and told him to get out of his father's house and leave his kindred and country to a land that He would show him.

> "Now the Lord had said unto Abram, Get thee out of thy country, and from thy kindred, and from thy father's house, unto a land that I will shew thee: And I will make of thee a great nation,

and I will bless thee, and make thy name great; and thou shalt be a blessing: And I will bless them that bless thee, and curse him that curseth thee: and in thee shall all families of the earth be blessed. So Abram departed, as the Lord had spoken unto him; and Lot went with him: and Abram was seventy and five years old when he departed out of Haran"

(Genesis 12:1-4).

God didn't tell Abraham where to go, yet the Bible says he launched out of his country, having no idea where he was going. He left by faith!

"By faith Abraham, when he was called to go out into a place which he should after receive for an inheritance, obeyed; and he went out, not knowing whither he went" (Hebrews 11:8).

Abraham lived as a pilgrim throughout his life because he knew by revelation that the Promised Land God spoke of wasn't a physical one but a spiritual one.

Also, when the Lord promised to give him a son in his old age, he believed. *"He staggered not at the promise of God through unbelief; but was strong in faith, giving glory to God"* (**Romans 4:20).** When God asked him to offer that son as a burnt sacrifice, he simply obeyed because he knew *"that God was able to raise him up, even from the dead"* (Hebrews 11:19).

That's what faith is all about - responding swiftly to God's instructions and doing everything He tells you. That's how you can please God in your life. Abraham was called 'the father of faith' and 'the friend of God' because he lived by faith in God's Word. This is the life to which we've been called as Christians – the faith life!

The Just Shall Live By Faith

> "Now the just shall live by faith:
> but if any man draw back, my soul
> shall have no pleasure in him"
> (Hebrews 10:38).

Everything in the Kingdom of God functions by the principle of faith. That's why the Bible says the just shall live by faith. It didn't say the just shall live by holiness or righteousness, but by faith. This shows just how important faith is and why the 'faith-message' should be taken very seriously by anyone who desires to live a successful life in God's Kingdom.

Everything about your life is hinged on your understanding of this important subject of faith. You can't understand righteousness without faith, just as it's impossible for you to demonstrate the God-kind of love without faith. The Bible says *"faith worketh by love"* (Galatians 5:6), love also works by faith.

Without faith, you wouldn't function well on your job, in your business, family, academics, finances, health or ministry. You can't even keep the devil under your feet where he belongs without faith!

In today's world, where there's so much evil and wickedness, you can only walk in love and live peaceably among all men as the Bible instructs to do, by faith. It takes faith to listen and not respond in bitterness when someone speaks evil of you. It takes faith to remain unruffled and still love those who criticize and despitefully use you. It takes faith to hold your head up and not let what your critics say cause you to react negatively. It takes faith not to wish evil for those who hate, mistreat and misjudge you.

You see, the faith way is the way, the only way for the Christian.

> "For I say, through the grace given unto me, to every man that is among you, not to think of

himself more highly than he ought to think; but to think soberly, according as GOD HATH DEALT TO EVERY MAN THE MEASURE OF FAITH"

(Romans 12:3).

Chapter Two

You Already Have Faith

Throughout the epistles, which actually are the revelations of the new creation, you'll never find a place where the Holy Spirit expressly instructs the Christian to have faith in God. The reason is quite simple: The just shall live by faith.

To the Christian, faith is a lifestyle. It is the New Testament principle of life for the believer. We are actually never told to have faith in God, because our very life is by faith. God already dealt to every man, according to the Scriptures, the measure of faith.

In other words, **you already have faith** as a Christian. The reason our Lord Jesus had to keep urging people around Him to have faith in God as found in Matthew, Mark and Luke is that those He was addressing at the time weren't born again.

If you are born again you have faith. God has given to every one of us in the body of Christ the measure of faith. Notice I didn't say *'a measure,'* but *'the measure'* of faith. That's because every Christian has faith. We have the exact amount of faith that we require to receive anything, and effect any change in our lives. What you need do is grow your measure of faith.

Faith Is Given To You – Small

As I said, when you're born again, you have faith! God imparts into your spirit the measure of faith.

However, that measure is given to you small. God doesn't give you big faith, He gives you little faith to enable you grow your faith. It's your responsibility to build your faith strong. The Bible talks about weak faith, little faith, great faith and strong faith. I'm going to be dealing with that in more detail in the sixth and seventh chapters but presently, the point I want you to note is that YOU ALREADY HAVE FAITH (the God-kind of faith), and that faith is given to you as small-initially.

You may say, "Oh, now I've discovered why my faith hasn't been working, it's because the faith God gave me is very small." Before you go further with that thought, let me remind you of the words of Jesus in Matthew 17:20. He said *"...for verily I say unto you, IF YE HAVE FAITH AS A GRAIN OF MUSTARD SEED, ye shall say unto this mountain, Remove hence to yonder place; and it shall remove; and <u>nothing shall be impossible unto you</u>.*

In other words, with your faith–the small measure of faith God has given to you, you should be able to do the impossible. You have in you the power to do anything. You can effect changes and control the circumstance of life to suit you if only you'll put your faith to work.

God gave you the exact amount of faith that He made available to everybody. He has never given any body any less than He gave to Jesus. We were all given the same measure of faith, but what matters is what we do with it.

You can be anything in this world! Understand this: you can have your life under control; your destiny isn't in the hands of anybody. You can go anywhere you choose to go; have every good thing you desire; live a supernatural life of prosperity and be an all-round success. How? It is by putting your faith to work, for faith always works!

Why then do some Christians' faith not work or yield result? Could the problem be sin?

The Problem Is Not Sin

Some people think the greatest problem in the body of Christ today is that of sin, but that's not true!

> "Knowing this, that our old man is crucified with him, that the body of sin might be destroyed, that henceforth we should not serve sin. For he that is dead is freed from sin"
>
> (Romans 6:6-7).

When you study the Bible carefully, you'll discover that the reason Jesus came to die was to deal with the problem of sin. As a believer, sin is no longer your problem. Many Christians struggle with sin in their lives because they are ignorant of God's Word. The death, burial and resurrection of Jesus Christ brought an end to sin and ushered the believer into a newness of life. That's why the Bible declares that *"...sin shall not have dominion over you"* (Romans 6:14).

You may say, "But so-and-so calls himself a Christian and still commits sin!" Yes, he may still commit sin, but you see, his problem is not the sin he's committing, but his ignorance. The devil sometimes tries to take advantage of this; he uses it to deceive God's children into believing that the reason they're not receiving from God is the sins they've committed. He makes them feel there are certain blessings they can't receive because of sin.

When you come to understand the nature and character of God, you'll discover He doesn't answer your prayer or bless you because you're living right, neither does He refuse to bless you because you're not. Living right is the desire of every child of God, for no true child of God will deliberately want to live in sin.

Every child of God desires to come out of anything that's wrong. That's one of the signs by which you can identify a child of God – he's uncomfortable with sin and doesn't want to continue in it. That's why when God looks at you He doesn't see your imperfection. As far as He's concerned, you're holy, unblameable and unreproveable in His sight (Colossians 1:21-22).

You may not feel righteous or holy all the time but this is the truth of God's Word about you. Your problem is not sin. You must understand this truth and let it soak into your mentality, otherwise it will be difficult for you to develop your faith and make it work.

When you understand that Jesus died for the propitiation of sin and He's given you a new life that's superior to satan, sin becomes a thing of the past. Jesus took responsibility, and paid the full penalty for your sins and misdeeds; past, present and future.

You Qualify For God's Best

The Bible admonishes us to *"...be strong in the*

grace that is in Christ Jesus" **(2 Timothy 2:1).** That means we should take advantage of God's unmerited favour! He has qualified us by Himself to be blessed. It is not our works but His own work on our behalf that has qualified us for this special place. That's what grace is all about, and Paul the Apostle encourages us to take advantage of it.

God has qualified you to be a partaker of the inheritance of the saints in light (Colossians 1:12). In other words, you're qualified to receive God's best, not because of your own works of righteousness but through the grace of Jesus Christ.

Some Christians have prayed unsuccessfully for many years to receive the Holy Spirit, to the point that they begin to doubt the authenticity of the Holy Spirit in others. Eventually, they conclude that what others have is not genuine.

In their search, they pray everyday, asking God to give them the Holy Spirit, but in spite of all their praying, they still haven't received Him. Their problem is not prayer, neither is it because they don't have faith! Their problem is they don't know how to receive!

They assumed they would receive the Holy Spirit on the basis of their good works. "I'm so holy, I rarely do anything wrong, yet I haven't received the Holy Spirit in spite of my praying for many years" that is their usual remark!

On the other hand, here is a scruffy-looking guy with earrings, probably on drugs and might have been drinking heavily too. However, somebody might talk to him about Jesus. He accepts the gospel and is born again. The next moment, he receives the Holy Spirit and starts talking in tongues. These other fellows who have been praying for years to receive the Holy Spirit may find this very confusing.

You need to know that receiving from God is not according to the works that we have done, but according to His grace. That grace is in Christ Jesus. He made us qualify to receive God's best! Hallelujah!

For your faith to work you must learn not to trust in your human ability or qualifications but in Christ. You must trust in the blood of Jesus Christ that speaks better things than the blood of Abel. He's the reason God cannot ***not*** bless you!

Settle this truth in your heart: **nothing can disqualify you from receiving God's best, not even your sins**! You're qualified to receive every good thing that God has made ready for all those who are in Christ Jesus. The Bible says, it's not of works, lest any man should boast but through the grace that's in Christ Jesus (Ephesians 2:8-9).

You may say, "But a sinner can't receive the blessings of God because God does not answer the prayer of sinners." Understand this: there's a great difference between the new creation and the unregenerate man. The new creation is not righteous because he does not sin, but because he is recreated in righteousness (Ephesians 4:24). When you're born again you're no longer a sinner but a saint. You become as righteous as God is righteous because

He gives you His very righteousness.

> "For he hath made him to be sin for us, who knew no sin; that we might be made the righteousness of God in him"
>
> (2 Corinthians 5:21).

So, if God is not going to answer the prayer of a sinner, that's not you. You're the righteousness of God in Christ Jesus. You're not a sinner. The sinner is the man who doesn't have the life and nature of God in Christ Jesus.

So, why then are many Christians praying and not receiving? Even though God has qualified us, and ordained us to receive answers when we pray, why aren't they receiving? The reason is they don't know how to receive!

Chapter Three

Jesus Taught Us How To Receive

Jesus gave the most profound teaching on the subject of faith. In **Mark 11:24**, He said,

> "Therefore I say unto you, what things soever ye desire, when ye pray, believe that ye receive them, and ye shall have them."

In this Scripture, He showed us how to pray and how to receive answers at the same time. However, too many Christians have stayed on one side of that scripture all their life–they've only learnt to pray, but haven't learnt to receive. They believe in praying alone, and that will not change anything. We need to know what to do to receive the answers to our prayers.

THE PRINCIPLE OF RECEIVING

Jesus said, *"...what things soever ye desire, when ye pray, BELIEVE THAT YE RECEIVE THEM, AND YE SHALL HAVE THEM."*

Jesus is teaching us how to receive in the latter part of this scripture. He's showing us the principle of receiving. In Matthew 7:8 He said, *"Everyone that asks receives."* In John 15:16, He lets us know we're chosen and ordained to receive answers when we pray:

> "I have chosen you, and ordained you ...that whatsoever ye shall ask of the Father in my name, he

may give it you."

Jesus never lied to anyone. He was always clear and succinct in His communication and never evasive. He said what He meant and meant what He said. On this occasion, He said, *"Everyone who asks, receives. Anyone who seeks, finds. If only you will knock, the door will be opened"* (Matthew 7:7-8 TLB).

What then is the problem with many folks? Why aren't they receiving? Prayer is of no use if there's no receiving. Praying without receiving is religion and religion gives you nothing.

So many people have come into Christianity with a religious mindset. They see prayer as an hour or a time of religious monologue; they spend a lot of time exerting themselves in prayer. But at the end of the day, they get frustrated because they aren't receiving answers. Of course, there are different kinds of prayers, and I have dealt with that in another book. Every prayer is not a request. However, we are dealing with requests in this book.

When you pray, God answers. Therefore all you need do is believe that you've received whatever it is you asked for. As I said, God answers when you pray, but you do the receiving. There's a faith attitude that determines whether you receive answers to your prayer or not.

Let's suppose you've prayed and asked God for a particular thing. If you truly believe the words of Jesus, after praying, you ought to rejoice immediately, congratulating yourself and declaring, "Wow! Thank you Jesus! Glory to God, I've got what I asked for!"

Even though your request is not seen with your physical eyes, you should act like you've already received it right from the moment you prayed. That's what Jesus said. That's the principle of receiving – you start acting and demonstrating your faith by rejoicing and giving God praise for your miracle.

Don't Complain, Just Receive!

Prayer is not an avenue to remind God about your needs and complain about all the things that are troubling you. Unfortunately, that's what many folks do. They complain instead of declaring the Word when they pray.

Jesus said when you pray, believe! He didn't say complain. He said believe. Believe what? That you've received! He went further to say "If you believe that you've received, that thing will show up - it will become yours." So, after praying, because you know you have received, begin to rejoice.

It's like someone who owns a car. He drives it to work, parks it in the parking lot and enters his office. While in the office, his car is certainly not by his side or anywhere in the office, but he has confidence and assurance that it is parked safely at the parking lot. He *knows* he has a car; it wouldn't make sense if he started acting as though he doesn't know he owns a car.

In the spirit, receiving from God is that way. You just *know* in your spirit that you have what you asked for when you prayed. At this time you're no longer trying to believe that you've received, rather you *know* that you have received. At the moment of prayer, you seem to know you GOT IT. You seem to actually ride that car as it were. But soon after the prayer, don't act like you lost it or never got it. Don't go about complaining or grumbling; you *know* in your spirit that you've already received, therefore keep the right attitude of faith.

When you understand this truth I'm sharing with you, you'll stop trying to get God to give you anything or do something for you. You really can't try to get Him to do anything for you anyway, since He's already done everything He ever needed to do for you. That's why He said *"all things are yours"* (1 Corinthians 3:21).

All God expects from you now is that you *receive* all things. Receive all that He says belongs to you in

His Word. When you receive God's Word of blessing into your spirit, it will certainly produce the blessing that it talks about in your life.

Maybe you've been praying to God for a child, a new job, or anything at all. After a while, you might begin to wonder or ask questions like "Should I keep asking or should I just believe that I've received?" No, don't believe you've received. Just receive! Once you've received something, you no longer need to believe that you've received it. It becomes yours the moment you receive it and you know it.

Chapter Four

Receiving Is By Faith

Hebrews 11:6 says without faith it's impossible to please God. Faith is the response of the human spirit to the Word of God. In other words, it's the step you take as a result of the Word of God that's come to you. God is a 'faith-God.'

Now, that's different from saying He's a 'faithful God.' When I say God is a 'faith-God,' I mean He lives and operates by faith, and He expects us, His kids, to do the same. God is a Spirit, and we are spirit beings as well. But we live in a physical and material world. Hence we must walk by faith.

I said earlier that when you pray, God answers you. **1 John 5:14-15** tells us,

> "...this is the confidence that we have in him, that, if we ask any thing according to his will, he heareth us: And if we know that he hear us, whatsoever we ask, we know that we have the petitions that we desired of him."

In other words, having prayed or asked God for something, your role is to begin to act as though He's done what you asked for because He's actually done it. That's the way to receive! You receive by accepting that God has done what He says He has done, and that you already have what He says you have. That's faith! Stop believing that God is going to do what you've asked Him; rather see that He's already done it and start acting that way. That's how to receive from God; that is faith.

It's Not Crying That Works; It's Faith!

Remember that true faith always works. If it didn't work, it wasn't faith. Whenever you respond to God by faith you'll surely receive a miracle. I always get inspired whenever I remember the testimony of a dear lady who got healed in one of our healing meetings.

She's been a Christian for many years but had become completely bed-ridden by sickness. Plus that, she suffered excruciating pains everyday. You couldn't even touch her, or she would writhe and cry out in pains. They had to make a wooden bed for her to lay flat on, which was used to carry her around.

In this condition, they brought her to the healing

school. When she was brought up to me at the platform to be prayed for, I perceived she had faith to be healed. Little wonder, the moment I prayed for her, she was healed instantly and she leapt out of that sickbed.

After her healing, whilst being interviewed, she explained how she came about her faith. She said she had listened repeatedly to some of the messages I preached on faith and prayer. She specifically mentioned the titles **'Two kinds of faith,' 'The God-kind of faith'** and **'Prevailing prayer**.' She said, "I listened to those tapes over and over again and that built my faith strong." She made another remarkable statement. She said, "I've been a Christian a long time, and I've been praying and crying to God to heal me. I cried everyday!"

But while listening to the tape titled ***Prevailing Prayer,*** she heard me say, "It's the effectual fervent prayer of a righteous man that avails much and not his effectual fervent crying." That message got to her thinking and she said, "I stopped crying."

She learnt from listening to that message that her constant crying everyday wasn't about to change her situation. Many of God's people need to realize this truth. Crying day and night about your pain isn't going to change anything. What you need is to act your faith. God didn't say the 'crying' of a righteous man avails much, but the 'prayer.'

> "The effectual fervent prayer of a righteous man availeth much"
>
> (James 5:16).

This means it's your prayer that produces result, not your crying. Now, don't get me wrong; I know about crying in prayer. I've preached a message titled ***'Try Tears'*** but that's not what I'm talking about here. I know there are times you pray and find yourself crying profusely in worship and supplication to God. That's a different thing all together.

This dear lady said she learnt that she didn't have to cry and beg God anymore to heal her as she'd done for six years. She said, "As I listened to Pastor

Chris' messages on faith, I came to understand the real meaning of the scripture that says *"By His stripes ye were healed.""* Her faith was already stirred up as she listened to God's Word on tape. So when I laid hands on her, she got up instantly healed by the power of God. Now she is teaching others about faith.

I want you to understand something: if you're born again, you don't need to suffer another day in your life. You don't have to be sick, broke, frustrated, poor, diseased or infirmed in your body. Put your faith to work! A glorious, prosperous, healthy, excellent, successful and good life is your God-given inheritance.

Remember, the Bible says *"...all things are yours..."* **(1 Corinthians 3:21).** That's talking about every good thing. Therefore receive your prosperity; receive your healing! Stop crying and begging God to do something about your case. He's already done everything He needed to do concerning your life and brought you into His place of health, wealth and glory in Christ Jesus.

2 Peter 1:3 tells us *"According as his divine power hath given unto us all things that pertain unto life and godliness, through the knowledge of him that hath called us to glory and virtue:"* His divine power has given you **ALL THINGS** that pertain unto life and godliness. This Scripture doesn't say He has given you **some things** that pertain to life, but ***all things***. All you need do now is receive all that's been made available to you in Christ.

Divine health is yours. Prosperity is yours. Lasting peace is yours. Success, excellence and the good life belong to you. Receive them into your spirit by believing, accepting and declaring them with your mouth; and watch your life transformed within a moment of time. This is how to receive by faith.

THE 'SAYING' PART OF RECEIVING!

"For verily I say unto you, That

> whosoever SHALL SAY unto this mountain, Be thou removed, and be thou cast into the sea; and shall not doubt in his heart, but shall believe that those things which he SAITH shall come to pass; HE SHALL HAVE WHATSOEVER HE SAITH" (Mark 11:23).

Stop crying and begging God to heal you. Instead, say, "I receive my healing!" Stop crying, "Oh God, save my husband!" Rather, declare that he's saved in the Name of Jesus, each time you pray for him, for the Word declares "thou shalt be saved and thy house" (Acts 16:31).

Stop praying "Oh God, give me a child!" say, "Father I thank You for I've received a child, because Your Word says children are the heritage of the Lord, and the fruit of the womb is His reward" (Psalm 127:3). Besides, the Bible says, *"You shall be blessed above all peoples; there shall not be a male or female barren among you or among your livestock"* **(Deuteronomy 7:14 NKJV).** Therefore it's impossible for you not to have children.

When you know this, you won't need to keep praying, begging or asking God to make you fruitful, or to give you a child. Instead, you'll simply go ahead and receive, Hallelujah!

Stop saying, "Oh God, give me money!" Instead, say, "I'm rich; I have all the money I need because God has made all favour and earthly blessings come to me in abundance. Therefore, I'm always, and under all circumstances, self-sufficient. I possess enough, to require no aid or support; and I'm financially furnished in abundance for every good work and charitable donation."

This should be your declaration! You can't talk like this everyday and be broke. It's impossible! You can't keep speaking like this and be in debt. The energy of God's Word will produce what it says in your life. **2 Corinthians 9:8 (AMP)** says,

> "God is able to make all grace (every favour and earthly blessing) come to you in abundance, so that you may always {and} under all circum-stances {and} whatever the need be self-sufficient [possessing enough to require no aid or support and furnished in abundance for every good work and charitable donation."

It's your responsibility to meditate, personalize and receive the blessings in God's Word by speaking in consonance with Him. That's the '*saying*' part of receiving.

For example, the Bible says, *"And my God will liberally supply (fill to the full) your every need according to His riches in glory in Christ Jesus"* **(Philippians 4:19 AMP).** I want you to notice it didn't say, "God will supply your needs according to how much money you have in your bank account," neither did it say, "God will supply your needs according to how good and stable the economy of the country where you live is." Rather it says, "*God will supply your every need according to His riches in glory by Christ Jesus.*"

Having come across this truth from God's Word, what's the next thing you should do? You start saying to yourself: "I refuse to lack or beg for money, for my God has liberally supplied my every need according to His riches in glory by Christ Jesus." When you talk like this, you put your faith to work. You're laying hold on your inheritance by faith. That's what faith does; it possesses!

When you're operating by the principles of faith, you don't say "Oh God make me rich!" If you're a Christian God is not going to make you rich, since He's already done it!

> "For ye know the grace of our
> Lord Jesus Christ, that, though

> he was rich, yet for your sakes he became poor, that YE THROUGH HIS POVERTY MIGHT BE RICH"
>
> (2 Corinthians 8:9).

You need to observe some beautiful truths in this Scripture. God is letting you know that you're not the poor trying to be rich; He's already made you rich. So, begin to declare your wealth with your mouth. This is the 'saying' part of receiving--you believe with your heart and *say* with your mouth all the wonderful things God has given to you, as stated in His Word.

Jesus said,

> **"For verily I say unto you, That whosoever shall say unto this mountain, Be thou removed, and be thou cast into the sea; and shall not doubt in his heart, but shall believe that those things**

which he saith shall come to pass;
he shall have whatsoever he saith"
(Mark 11:23).

He lets us know, as evident in the latter part of this Scripture that **"What you say, is what you get."**

Speaking or saying with your mouth what God says belongs to you in His Word, is a key to your receiving. It's a key to making your faith work.

Faith Receives

Once again, let's look at the words of Jesus in **Matthew 7:7-8:**

"ASK, and IT SHALL BE GIVEN YOU; seek, and ye shall find; knock, and it shall be opened unto you: For every one that asketh RECEIVETH; and he that seeketh findeth; and to him that knocketh it shall be opened."

These words are the sovereign declarations of Deity – they are absolute truths! Note the manner in which the Lord conjoins asking (or praying) with receiving. The Master is not only interested in your praying but also in your receiving. He said everyone that asks, receives, and that includes you. Now, that's a law in the realm of the spirit. It's an established principle in the Kingdom of God to which you belong – **you're ordained to receive answers to prayer.**

The Bible didn't say He that begs or cries out to God, receives. A lot of God's children are praying and begging God to give them what the Bible already says belongs to them. If only they would stop begging and start receiving! Let me tell you something about faith: faith doesn't beg; faith receives!

Remember what I told you earlier: praying without receiving is religion and religion gives you nothing; but faith receives all things, Hallelujah! Don't be religious in your thinking. Don't spend a lot of time exerting yourself in prayer without understanding how to receive. It will only lead to frustrations.

Jesus said about the religious folks, *"...they think that they shall be heard for their much speaking"* (Matthew 6:7). You need to know that the volume of your words when you pray is not what moves God; it's your faith that gets His attention. Believing and accepting that what He says is yours is yours; what He says He has done, He has done; and therefore acting that way is what faith is all about.

Faith is believing, endorsing and receiving God's Word as the ONLY truth. Your faith won't work when you merely stop at believing what the Bible says. Faith believes, receives and therefore speaks. Faith is a possessor! You must always substantiate your believing by adding something to it; and that's the faith-action, which is demonstrated by your speaking.

Jesus said about the religious folks, "...they think that they shall be heard for their much speaking" (Matt. 6:7). [illegible] know that we [illegible] require [illegible]

Faith, believing, and [illegible] and [illegible] [illegible]. [illegible]

Chapter Five

Two Kinds Of Faith

Some of the most profound and inspiring words ever spoken by the Master on the subject of faith are found in Mark's gospel, chapter eleven, from the twenty-second into the twenty-fourth verse:

> "And Jesus answering saith unto them (His disciples) HAVE FAITH IN GOD. For verily I say unto you, That whosoever shall

> say unto this mountain, Be thou removed, and be thou cast into the sea; and shall not doubt in his heart, but shall believe that those things which he saith shall come to pass; he shall have whatsoever he saith. Therefore I say unto you, What things soever ye desire, when ye pray, believe that ye receive them, and ye shall have them."

Jesus instructs in verse 22, *"Have faith in God."* When you read that verse, using a good marginal reference Bible, you'll see that what Jesus actually said was, *"Have the faith of God."* In other words, *"Have the God-kind of faith."* So, there's the *God-kind* of faith!

The other type is the human-kind of faith. The human-kind of faith is based on knowledge or information obtained from the senses, that is, sensory perception. It is sense-knowledge faith, thus, it is really not faith in the actual sense, since faith is the evidence of things not seen or perceived with the senses (Hebrews 11:1).

We can find in the Bible someone who operated this kind of faith. His name was Thomas, one of the twelve disciples of Jesus. This is the reason human or sense-knowledge faith is sometimes referred to as the *'Thomas-kind of faith.'*

Therefore, in the general sense, there are two kinds of faith: *the God-kind of faith* and *the human-* or *Thomas-kind of faith.*

THE 'GOD-KIND OF FAITH' VERSUS THE 'THOMAS-KIND' OF FAITH

> "Now faith is the substance of things hoped for, the EVIDENCE OF THINGS NOT SEEN"
>
> (Hebrews 11:1).

In the light of this scriptural definition of faith,

the *Thomas-kind of faith* is actually not faith. This is because it believes, and calls real only the things that the physical senses can perceive. It only calls real, things that can be seen, felt or touched physically. It's the kind of faith that says, "Except I see with my eyes, I'll not believe!" This kind of faith does not produce any result; it gives you nothing. Moreover, operating in it cannot give you any blessing.

When Thomas was told by the other disciples that the Master was alive and they had seen Him (this was after His crucifixion), he blurted, "Except I see the nail prints in his hands and put my fingers in those nail holes, and see the wound in his side where that Roman soldier thrust a spear through, I will not believe!"

A few days after he made this statement, the disciples were gathered together in a room with the doors shut, and suddenly Jesus appeared to them again. This time Thomas was present at the meeting. Jesus turned to Thomas and said to him,

> "...reach hither thy finger, and behold my hands; and reach hither thy hand, and thrust it into my side: and be not faithless, but believing. And Thomas answered and said unto him, My Lord and my God. Jesus saith unto him, Thomas, because thou hast seen me, thou hast believed: BLESSED ARE THEY THAT HAVE NOT SEEN, AND YET HAVE BELIEVED"
>
> (John 20:26-29).

Jesus knew Thomas' remark, although He wasn't physically present when he made his comment. However, when He appeared the second time to His disciples, He came specifically for Thomas.

The Bible says, *"And Thomas answered and said unto him, My Lord and my God"* (John 20:28). In other words, "I've seen you, so now I believe!" But

Jesus wasn't moved by his word; He wasn't impressed with Thomas' faith. He said, *"Thomas, because thou hast seen me, thou hast believed: blessed are they that have not seen, and yet have believed"* (John 20:29).

The next time you hear someone say, "I must see first, before I believe," that person is operating the Thomas-Kind of faith. According to the words of Jesus, he or she is not blessed. The one who's blessed is the one who believes before seeing.

The Thomas-kind of faith gives you nothing; it doesn't work! It doesn't produce any spiritual results. Does this apply to you? Are you one of those who say things like, "How can I say I'm rich when there's no money in my pocket and bank account?" Or "How can I say I'm healed when I can still feel pain in my body?" Don't ask such silly questions. Have you forgotten the Bible says "Faith is the substance of things hoped for, THE EVIDENCE OF THINGS NOT SEEN?"

The evidence you need to prove that you're healthy and prosperous is God's Word. The Bible says,

> "For ye know the grace of our Lord Jesus Christ, that, though he was rich, yet for your sakes he became poor, that ye through his poverty might be rich"
>
> (2 Corinthians 8:9).

And in 1 Peter 2:24, it says,

> "Who his own self bare our sins in his own body on the tree, that we, being dead to sins, should live unto righteousness: BY WHOSE STRIPES YE WERE HEALED."

These are evidences from God's Word that guarantee your health and financial prosperity. If you're waiting to have your pocket and bank account filled with a lot of money before you declare you're rich, then it means you don't believe God's Word. You have the Thomas-kind of faith.

Have you ever heard someone say, "Unless I see a miracle, I will not believe?" Even after seeing a miracle, such folks will still demand proofs and verifications to believe such miracles are of God. I would to God such folks would realize their ignorance and come to know that miracles are not subject to scientific or empirical proofs. The unfortunate thing about this group of people is they claim to be smarter than everybody else.

Just like Thomas, when they hear a testimony about someone who was healed of a terminal disease, for example, they'll say, "You think I'm a fool? Unless I see a proof from the doctors, confirming this person no longer suffers from that sickness, I will not believe." They'll tell you, "I'm a realist; I only believe what I see, feel or touch." What a shame!

Don't believe what you see, believe what God says! That's faith, and that's the faith that **works**! Somebody said, "I work with facts and figures." Don't work with facts and figures; walk by faith, based on God's Word.

Many folks today are having problems in their faith walk because they operate the *Thomas-kind of faith* which in scriptural sense is not faith at all. When Jesus rebuked Thomas in John 20:27, He said to him "**...be NOT FAITHLESS, but believing...**" which means Thomas was actually faithless! He exhibited no faith at all – he had *zero-faith*. Don't be that way!

One time, Jesus rebuked His disciples and asked them, *"...Why are you so fearful? how is it that ye have no faith?"* (Mark 4:40). He chided them for their lack of faith! So there's zero faith, and that's the Thomas or sense-knowledge kind of faith.

However, Jesus counsels us to have the God-kind of faith. That's the faith that works and produces result. That's the kind of faith we're expected to operate as believers. That's the faith that's already been given to every Christian by God.

Romans 12:3 lets us know we have this faith already:

> "For I say, through the grace given unto me, to every man that is among you, not to think of himself more highly than he ought to think; but to think soberly, according as GOD HATH DEALT TO EVERY MAN THE MEASURE OF FAITH."

You have the God-kind of faith in you. You're required to put it to work. Use it. The more you put it to work, the stronger it becomes. You don't have to pray to have the God-kind of faith; if you're born again you already have the God-kind of faith.

Chapter Six

Little Faith And Great Faith

Remember that I said when we speak generically of faith, we can say there are two kinds of faith: **the God-kind of faith** and **the human** or **Thomas-kind of faith,** which in the light of the scriptures, is really not faith.

However, for the God-kind of faith, there are actually four different categories the Bible recognizes. These four kinds (or classifications) of faith are: **little faith**, **weak faith**, **great faith** and **strong faith**.

The Lord Jesus talked about great faith and little faith. Once, He said to His disciples *"O ye of little faith"* (Matthew 8:26). On another occasion, He commended the Roman Centurion, whose servant was sick, for exhibiting great faith. He said to him, *"... I have not found so great faith, no, not in Israel"* (Luke 7:9).

The Apostle Paul talked about the other two: ***weak faith*** and ***strong faith***. In Romans 4:19, talking about Abraham, he said, *"And being not weak in faith, he considered not his own body now dead..."* Another version says, *"He did not exercise weak faith."* Then in the twentieth verse, he said Abraham *"...was strong in faith, giving glory to God;"*

This chapter's focus is on little faith and weak faith. I'll show you the causes and characteristics of these two kinds of faith and the cures for them.

Little Faith

Remember that if you're born again, you already have faith – the God-kind of faith. In Romans 12:3 Paul declares,

> "For I say, through the grace given unto me, to every man that is among you, not to think of himself more highly than he ought to think; but to think soberly, ACCORDING AS GOD HATH DEALT TO EVERY MAN THE MEASURE OF FAITH."

I want you to observe that in this verse of scripture, the Apostle Paul is not writing to sinners or the world but to Christians. He said, *"For I say through the grace given unto me to every man that is **among you...**"* He wasn't talking to everybody in the world but to those '***among you.***' Who are these?

The saints! God has dealt to every born-again believer the measure of faith.

Notice also that he didn't say "*a* measure of faith," but "*the* measure of faith." That is quite significant and it means it's the same measure (size or quantity) of faith every believer receives from God at salvation. Now, that deposit of faith is given to you small, but God expects you to grow it.

It's your responsibility to increase the measure of faith God has given to you, and the way to do that is by learning more of God's Word. Your faith will increase as you hear God's Word, for *"...faith cometh by hearing, and hearing by the word of God"* (Romans 10:17).

The more of God's Word you hear, the more faith you'll have. The less of God's Word you receive into your spirit, the less faith you'll be able to express when you're faced with the challenges of life. The reason you must grow your faith is that LITTLE FAITH WILL NOT GET THE JOB DONE!

The reason fear grips people in the face of adversity is that their faith is little. The Bible says, **"If thou faint in the day of adversity, thy strength is small" (Proverbs 24:10).** Here, the Bible is not talking about your physical strength or muscles; it's referring to your faith! When your faith is little you'll faint; you'll give up in the day of trouble.

Jesus was in the ship with His disciples one day when a violent storm arose. The Bible tells us He was sleeping while His disciples battled the waves pouring in and threatening to sink the ship. After they'd tried all they could and the storm seemed to get worse, they rushed to Him and shook Him awake, shouting, *"Lord, save us! We perish"* (Matthew 8:25). Mark's account tells us they said, *"...Teacher, don't you care that we're about to drown?"* (Mark 4:38 CEV).

When Jesus woke up, He was unruffled. He didn't jump up in fear. He simply got up and rebuked the winds and the sea, and said, "Peace be still!" and there was a great calm! Then He turned to His disciples and said to them, "*Why are ye fearful, O ye of little faith*?" (Matthew 8:26). When your faith is little, you'll be oppressed and tormented by fear of circumstances, hence your faith will not work. Faith and fear don't go together. Fear hinders faith, but faith destroys fear.

The reason some Christians find themselves doubting God's Word is that their faith is little. Remember, little faith will not get the job done. It may get it started, but it won't get it done! What do I mean?

I'll illustrate with this example. Jesus had just finished preaching in the desert and performing the miracle of feeding five thousand men (women and children not counted) with five loaves and two fishes. Then He instructed His disciples to go ahead of Him by ship to the other side of the Sea of Galilee.

Shortly after they set out, their ship ran into contrary winds and was tossed about by the waves. To worsen things, at about the fourth watch (between

3 and 6 a.m.), they saw a figure approaching them on the water. The Bible says when Peter and the other disciples saw this, they all screamed in fear because they thought they had seen a ghost:

> "And when the disciples saw him walking on the sea, they were troubled, saying, It is a spirit; and they cried out for fear. But straightway Jesus spake unto them, saying, Be of good cheer; it is I; be not afraid. AND PETER ANSWERED HIM AND SAID, LORD, IF IT BE THOU, BID ME COME UNTO THEE ON THE WATER. And he said, Come. And when Peter was come down out of the ship, he walked on the water, to go to Jesus. But when he saw the wind boisterous, he was afraid; and beginning to sink, he cried,

saying, Lord, save me"
(Matthew 14:26-30).

Notice this statement Peter made to Jesus: "If it's You, ask me to come to You on the water." Jesus called to him and said "Come!" Peter came out of the ship and walked on the water to Jesus. He didn't swim in the water to meet Jesus, he walked on it! As a fisherman, he could swim, however, this time he did something supernatural, he walked on the water. He stepped out of the boat, right on the water and took his steps toward the Master, because the Master had said to him, "Come!" That's faith!

I would like to draw your attention to the thirtieth verse. It says, *"... when he (Peter) saw the wind boisterous, he was afraid; and beginning to sink, he cried, saying, Lord, save me."*

Peter saw the contrary wind and became afraid. As a result, he started sinking right in the presence of Jesus. Why did Peter begin to sink? What happened to the faith that got him out of the boat and started him out walking on water? The answer is in Jesus' response to his cry for help:

> "And immediately Jesus stretched forth his hand, and caught him, and said unto him, O thou of little faith, wherefore didst thou doubt?"
>
> (Verse 31).

Peter's faith was little, that was why he began to sink. Remember, I said little faith will not get the job done. It may get it started, but it won't finish it. It got Peter out of the boat and put him on the water; it even started him walking on it but couldn't sustain him when the winds became boisterous.

When the contrary winds and adversities of life begin to blow in your face, your strength will fail if your faith is little. Little faith achieves very little. When your faith is little you can be terrorized by fear. You'll always fear adversity and be uncertain about the future.

This is what happened to Peter. Fear and doubt

gripped his heart when he saw the boisterous winds. But thank God he had enough sense to cry out to Jesus for help and *"...immediately Jesus stretched forth his hand, and caught him..."* (Matthew 14:31).

Jesus attributed the reason Peter began to sink to doubt. After saving him from drowning, He said to him, *"O thou of little faith, wherefore didst thou doubt?"* In other words, if Peter had not doubted, he would have completed his walk on the water to Jesus and back to the boat hitch-free. Doubt and fear are the result of little faith.

If your faith is little, what is responsible for it and what can you do about it? Let's find out.

Little faith is the result of insufficient information. Hosea 4:6 says *"My people are destroyed for lack of knowledge..."* God Himself said this about His own people. He said His children - Christians, are destroyed, that is, they suffer, are impoverished, punished, brought down, crushed and perish because they lack the knowledge of His Word.

However, the more of God's Word you hear, the more knowledge you have, and faith comes to you in the Word. The less of God's Word you hear, the less faith you have.

Great Faith

To a woman of Canaan, a Syrophoenician by birth, Jesus responded in Matthew 15:28 *"O woman,* ***great is thy faith****: be it unto thee even as thou wilt."* Great faith is tenacious faith. It is faith that will not give up in spite of opposition. It is faith that responds with knowledge. This type of faith is based on the amount and quality of information you have received, accepted and endorsed.

When Jesus tested the woman's faith by telling her that what she desired could not be hers, as circumstances would many times tell you, she responded with knowledge. She spoke back words of faith. Read again this inspiring dialogue between Jesus and the woman:

"And, behold, a woman of Canaan came out of the same coasts, and cried unto him, saying, Have mercy on me, O Lord, thou Son of David; my daughter is grievously vexed with a devil. But he answered her not a word. And his disciples came and besought him, saying, Send her away; for she crieth after us. But he answered and said, I am not sent but unto the lost sheep of the house of Israel. Then came she and worshipped him, saying, Lord, help me. But he answered and said, It is not meet to take the children's bread, and to cast it to dogs. And she said, Truth, Lord: yet the dogs eat of the crumbs which fall from their masters' table. Then Jesus

> answered and said unto her, O woman, great is thy faith: be it unto thee even as thou wilt. And her daughter was made whole from that very hour"
>
> (Matthew 15:22-28).

When Jesus heard her informed answer, He said to her, *"...woman, great is thy faith."*

On another occasion, Jesus said the same thing about a Roman Centurion in Luke 7:9;

> "When Jesus heard these things, he marvelled at him, and turned him about, and said unto the people that followed him, I say unto you, I have not found so great faith, no, not in Israel."

The Master's words were again, a response to the words spoken by the lips of faith. Remember, the more accurate information you have, the better.

And when you act undauntedly on this information, you will be demonstrating great faith or 'much faith' as it were.

Romans 10:17 says, *"So then faith cometh by hearing, and hearing by the word of God."* So you see, when you don't have enough spiritual information from the Word about a particular issue, your faith will be little as your faith is according to God's Word that you've heard. The cure for such little faith therefore is simply to learn more of God's Word on that issue. The Scripture we just read tells us how faith comes – by hearing God's Word.

If you have any situation that seems hopeless, get into the Word! Become a student of the Word by careful and diligent search and study on the scriptures that talk about your peculiar situation. Get the teaching tapes and books that are relevant to your situation.

If you're having problems in your health or finances, or with getting a job or expanding your business, or in your academics as a student, or in any area of your life, this is what you should do. Get more information from God's Word. Inundate your spirit and bombard your mind with God's Word. Get teaching tapes in audio and video formats; listen to them and watch them again and again. Don't say, "I've already listened to the tapes." Keep listening!

I've listened to certain tapes through the years over and over again. I have tapes that are more than ten years old and I've listened to them repeatedly. God's Word never grows old; it's undated. As you keep listening to it, your mind, your thinking and mindset will begin to change and align with God's vision for your life.

God's Word is Spirit. It has the divine capacity to stir you up, give you a vision, energize you for success and programme you for greatness. Don't underestimate the power of God's Word.

When you face challenges, put the tapes on and keep listening! Listen until the Word gets into your spirit and renews your mind! Listen until your thinking, ideas and perspective change! That's the cure for little faith. That's how to grow your faith big.

Chapter Seven

Weak Faith And Strong Faith

WEAK FAITH

"And being not weak in faith, he considered not his own body now dead, when he was about an hundred years old, neither yet the deadness of Sarah's womb:" (Romans 4:19).

Weak faith is the result of the ***lack of exercise*** of faith or the ***non-exercise of faith***. What does that mean? When you hear God's Word, and don't act upon it, your faith will be weak. Remember, I said little faith is the result of insufficient information from God's Word, but weak faith is the result of not acting on the information you have.

Have you ever heard someone say, "I know the Bible says so, but let's face reality!" What could be more real than the Word of God? God's Word is absolute reality! Reality means truth and God's Word is truth (John 17:17).

I always get amazed at folks who say they know the Bible says something, yet they're not acting on it. For example, a Christian says, "I know the Bible says *"by His stripes we were healed"* but he's lying down sick. You say to him, "Brother, the Bible says you were healed, so act on the Word by proclaiming your healing!"

Then he responds, "Just give me some time. I know the Bible says so, but this pain is too much. I can't even place my feet on the ground; my head is aching seriously..." You see, he can quote the scriptures, he can even preach it, but he's not acting on it.

That's weak faith. You say you know it, but you're not acting on it! You're considering the pain instead of acting on God's Word. You have the information, from God's Word, and not only can you quote it, you can even teach it and share it with others, but you're not doing it. Your faith will be weak and when you face the crisis of life, it will not work. Your weak faith will cause you to stagger, and as a result, fear will grip you and you'll be defeated by the crisis of life. Then you'll begin to wonder, *"Why did God do this to me?"* God didn't do it to you. It was your faith that couldn't carry you. Your faith didn't work because it was weak!

Look at what the Bible says about Abraham, *"He staggered not at the promise of God through unbelief; but was STRONG IN FAITH, giving glory to God"* (Romans 4:20). He **staggered** or **wavered** not at the promise of God. When your faith is weak, you'll waver and stagger. You'll ask for proof before you can believe God's Word.

There you are praying or talking to God about

something, and suddenly you receive a prophecy concerning it. You hear God say, "*Cheer up. I've already done what you're asking for.*" Then you begin to rejoice because in your spirit, you sense the note of victory. But outwardly, it doesn't look as though anything has changed in line with the word of prophecy you got from God.

A few days or even weeks later, you start wondering, "I know God said it, but nothing has changed." You now start praying and asking God for the same thing all over again as though you never prayed about it before. You even start asking everybody to help you pray. Now you're praying and asking for something God already gave you a rhema-word about; something He told you He's done already. That's unbelief. Your faith can't work that way!

You got the information, but you haven't acted on it. That's weak faith. So what is the cure for weak faith?

Curing Weak Faith

The cure for weak faith is acting on the Word – acting on the information you've received. If you want your faith to be great and strong, START DOING THE WORD!

For example, the Bible says, *"In every thing give thanks: for this is the will of God in Christ Jesus concerning you"* (1 Thessalonians 5:18). So what should you do? Start practising that scripture in your life – give thanks in every situation! Let your life become an unending stream of praise and thanksgiving to God. Irrespective of what happens, you'll always say "Thank You Jesus;" you praise Him in everything! That's acting on the Word!

You see, the more you exercise your faith, the stronger your faith gets, and the way to exercise your faith is by acting on the Word. You tell yourself, "The Word of God says, "By *His stripes we were healed,"* therefore, I refuse to be sick. I'm not the sick trying to be healed! Sickness, disease and infirmity have no place in my body. Therefore, I refuse to lie down in bed sick or remain in this wheel-chair or go about with crutches, for I am the healed of the Lord, because the Word says so!"

That's acting on the Word. You take God's Word as the only truth and final arbiter in every circumstance of life. You refuse to be deterred by anything that's not consistent with God's Word.

For your faith to become strong and not weak, and to produce results, you must be a ***doer*** of the Word – you must practise the Word. As Christians, we're Word-practitioners. We practise the Word because God's Word is practicable.

So when the Bible says, for example, in Philippians 4:6-7, *"Be anxious for nothing, but in everything, by prayer and supplication, with thanksgiving, let your request be made known unto God and the peace of God that surpasses all understanding shall guard your hearts and minds through Christ Jesus,"* you practise it.

You practise exactly what that Word says in your life. First, you say to yourself: "I refuse to fear, I reject anxiety." Then you go ahead and make your request known to God and receive peace into your heart. From then on, you refuse to complain, murmur, act or think as if the devil has the upper hand in anything that concerns you. Everyday, you give God praise because you know He's granted your heart's desires. That's faith!

That way, you're exercising your faith and building your faith muscles. Some people know how to build their physical shape. Have you ever seen some of those well-trained, very athletic macho-looking guys? They spend a lot of time in the gym keeping in shape and building their muscles by exercising frequently. They run, jog, do press-ups and push-ups, all in the bid to build a strong, healthy, fit and agile physical body.

Do you realize this is the same manner you build your spirit as well? Just as lack of physical exercise makes your muscles weak, so also does lack of the faith-exercise makes your faith muscles weak. Without exercising yourself, your body may be big but weak. The same way, your faith may appear much but weak, if you don't exercise it by doing the Word. You must become a Word-practitioner.

For instance, Jesus said in Mark 11:24, "*Therefore I say unto you, What things soever ye desire, when ye pray, believe that ye receive them, and ye shall have them.*" That means, when you pray or ask God for anything, all you need do is believe that you've received them, and they are yours.

In other words, having prayed and asked God to grant you a particular request, (maybe a new job) you should immediately begin to testify and give God praise because your request has been granted. Your confession becomes: "Thank you Jesus; I've got what I asked for. Jesus said, "Whatsoever things I desire when I pray, I should believe that I receive them and I shall have them. I believe I've received a new job; therefore I have a new job, glory to God!"

That's how to act on the Word. You say to yourself, "Against hope, I believe in hope that I have a new job;" irrespective of what you hear, see or how you feel!

You may even have gone for a job interview and have been rejected; yet you refuse to be frustrated or despondent. You refuse to endorse such a verdict or allow it daunt your faith. You maintain your stand on God's Word and keep declaring "I have a new job! God gave it to me when I prayed and I received it." Before long, that job will show up. Even if it never existed, it'll be created because of you. That's what the Word says.

This is the kind of attitude you must have after praying and asking God for anything. Some people, after praying, instead of rejoicing and giving God praise for answering their prayers begin to look forlorn and depressed as though they were whipped by God for daring to ask Him for something. That's not the faith attitude. Remember I said earlier, there's a faith attitude, and that's the attitude that tells whether or not you received whatever it was you asked for when you prayed.

The way to develop your faith and build it strong is by putting it to work that's how to exercise your faith muscles. Until your faith is strong, it won't produce much results; and for your faith to be strong you must exercise it by acting on the Word; you must act your believing!

When you start out acting on God's Word, you may find yourself making some mistakes, but I want you to know that God has made allowance for your mistakes. He knows you're learning. So, don't get discouraged or frustrated about the mistakes you make in your journey of faith with God. Keep acting on the Word.

For example, maybe the first time you tried to preach the gospel and lead someone to Christ, you thought you didn't quite get it right. You got into an argument with the person and couldn't make a head-way in getting the fellow to give his heart to Christ.

Don't get discouraged by that. Keep exercising your faith muscles in that area by preaching the gospel again and again at every opportunity.

There are Christians who have never led someone to Christ, and they've been Christians a long time, maybe ten years or even more. That's sad. They can't think of a single person they've led to Christ, yet they believe if they spoke to someone about Jesus, he would be saved, but they've never done it! Why? They haven't exercised their faith in that area yet.

Imagine you saying to yourself in all honesty and sincerity, "I'm going to talk to someone today about Jesus. I'm going to win a soul to Christ today!" You get on the bus to work or school or wherever you're going, and there you meet someone. As you're about to open your mouth to preach, your heart begins to pound. You start debating within yourself, "Should I say something, or should I not? How do I begin? What if he doesn't listen to me?"

Whilst debating within yourself on how to begin, what to say and how to say it, the man gets off at the next stop. Of course, you'll feel bad and regret your failure to act. But let me tell you what to do the next time you have such an opportunity: Use it! Don't debate within yourself whether or not to speak; don't ask yourself "How do I start?" Just start! You say what if I make a mistake? Make it; but start. That's how to exercise your faith and put it to work; you dare to take your step according to God's Word!

A learner does not become perfect without mistakes, but work your way to perfection. Tell yourself, "I'm going to trust the Holy Spirit; I'll depend on Him to help me." Then you'll remember that the Bible says, "*Open your mouth wide and I will fill it*" (Psalm 81:10). So, you go ahead, open your mouth and begin to speak. You'll be amazed because the Holy Spirit will give you the right words to speak. He will also help you minimize your errors as you allow Him guide you.

Start winning souls, and as you do, your faith

will be strengthened. When you begin talking to people about Jesus, your faith will become stronger for the next time. Seize the next opportunity and talk to someone about Jesus, you'll be amazed how your faith has become strengthened overnight.

Start doing the things you really want to do that are in line with God's Word. The more you do them the stronger your faith will become. You develop and strengthen your physical muscles by exercising them.

You just can't keep sleeping and eating and expect your muscles to get stronger. They will never get strong that way. They only get stronger by exercise. That's the same thing with faith. Your faith will become great and strong and produce greater results because you're exercising it.

Have you ever seen a big fellow with weak muscles? He's huge but he's weak. What's he supposed to do? Eat more? No! He got that big from eating. Now his body is big but that doesn't mean it's strong. You tell him to run a few yards and he can't. He can't do anything a little exerting without panting heavily, but he's big.

How can he become fit and strong? He needs to be engaged in more physical activities; he needs to involve himself in physical exercises. That way, his big, weak body will become strong. The way that guy grew large from eating is the same way your faith increases by hearing – *eating* God's Word. By feeding on God's Word you grow your faith big. Know that even though your faith is great, it can't do anything if it's weak faith. For your great faith to work, it's got to be strong faith.

Strong Faith

God tells us something beautiful about Abraham in Romans 4:19-20; He says,

> **"And being not weak in faith, he considered not his own body now**

dead, when he was about an hundred years old, neither yet the deadness of Sarah's womb: He staggered not at the promise of God through unbelief; but was STRONG IN FAITH, giving glory to God."

This portion of scripture lets us know the kind of faith Abraham demonstrated that made him God's friend and the father of faith! He demonstrated strong faith in God's Word. He staggered not at the promise-the Word of God, through unbelief; He was "***strong in faith, giving glory to God***." This immediately lets us know that one of the characteristics of strong faith is, it gives glory to God.

When your faith is strong, it's very easy for you to believe whatever God tells you in His Word. You're quick to believe once you hear God's Word! Not only are you quick to believe, you also begin to glorify and worship God because you know that His

Word that you've believed, accepted, and endorsed has already come to pass in your life.

This is the faith that never fails. It's an unqualified, unrivalled, irrevocable committal to God and His Word. You cast yourself on God, taking His Word as the absolute truth. You hinge your believing on His eternal and unfailing Word only. When this becomes your resolve and the way you live your life, your faith will be strong and productive! Strong faith is the faith that works.

When Jesus told His disciples to **"Have the God-kind of faith,"** He was teaching His disciples and, of course, the rest of us as well to have strong faith. Jesus didn't say, *"Well, try to grow your faith,"* neither did He say, *"I know your faith is still weak, but one day it'll get strong."* Rather, He said, *"Have the God-kind of faith,"* not the "Thomas-kind of faith;" not "little faith," or "weak faith" but strong faith!

Strong faith is the faith that speaks, and it comes to pass! That's the faith God used in creating the heavens and the earth. The Bible says in Genesis 1:1, *"In the beginning God created the heavens and the earth."* He did it by speaking words of faith! He spoke, and what He said came into being.

Everything that exists, everything that we see today, the sun, the moon, the stars, all, except man, came into existence that way. When He said, *"Let there be light,"* light came into existence (Genesis 1:3).

Every Word God spoke during the creation came to pass because He spoke in faith. God is a faith God. He believed; He knew that whatever He said would come to pass. That's strong faith. Jesus defined strong faith in Mark 11:23 when He said,

> "For verily I say unto you, That whosoever shall say unto this mountain, Be thou removed, and be thou cast into the sea; and shall not doubt in his heart, but SHALL BELIEVE THAT

THOSE THINGS WHICH HE SAITH SHALL COME TO PASS; HE SHALL HAVE WHATSOEVER HE SAITH."

In Mark 11:12 He was hungry and wanted to eat some fruits. Seeing a fig tree afar off, He thought He could get some fruits out of it to assuage his hunger. On getting to the tree, there were no fruits but leaves only, because it wasn't time for figs. Then Jesus spoke to the tree and said, *"No man eat fruit of thee hereafter for ever. And his disciples heard it"* (Mark 11:14). His disciples heard Him when He spoke to the tree. Meaning He wasn't talking in His mind; He spoke audibly, such that His disciples that were present with Him, heard what He said.

Now, after Jesus talked to the tree, it looked the same as it was before He talked to it. But twenty-four hours later, His disciples observed that the fig tree had dried up from the roots, which clearly suggests that when Jesus talked to the tree, it died immediately from the roots.

The roots were in the ground, so no one could immediately tell that anything had happened to the tree. More so, everything else looked the same (the branches, the stem, the leaves, etc). Meanwhile, the tree was already dead from the root. Its source of life had been cut off.

Seeing that the tree had withered away, the disciples were amazed. Then Peter said, "Master, look! The tree you cursed has withered away." It was in response to Peter's statement that Jesus said to His disciples, *"Have the faith of God;"* meaning, "Have the 'God-kind' of faith." He wanted them to know that with this kind of faith, they could do anything.

Just like Jesus when He spoke to the fig tree, each time you release words of faith, whether or not you feel or see any change wouldn't make any difference. In your spirit, you know that the words you've spoken with your mouth will surely come to pass. Strong faith does not give consideration to the outward appearance of things. First, I said it gives glory to God. Secondly, it doesn't consider the circumstances.

Don't Consider The Circumstances

The Bible says Abraham CONSIDERED NOT his own body now dead, when he was about an hundred years old, neither did he consider the deadness of Sarah's womb: He staggered not at the promise of God through unbelief; but was STRONG IN FAITH, giving glory to God (Romans 4:19).

Abraham was a hundred years old when God told him he was going to have a son and call his name Isaac. Though he was already well stricken in age, he refused to consider his body as dead; as being unable to reproduce! Neither did he consider the fact that Sarah's womb was dead. He was undeterred by every physical and natural evidence that challenged the ability of God.

Everything that he knew in this world, told him it was impossible for him to have a child. His body as far as reproducing was concerned, was dead. He was about a hundred years old, Sarah had been pronounced barren. Yet, Abraham didn't consider the deadness of Sarah's womb. What then was Abraham considering? He was considering the Word. He gave thought, attention and focus only to the Word that God had spoken to him.

As far as Abraham was concerned, God said it; and He was well able to bring it to pass. That's strong faith; when you refuse to consider anything else but God's Word that has come to you.

That Abraham didn't consider his body or the deadness of Sarah's womb doesn't mean he didn't see his body; or he didn't know that Sarah his wife was barren. He saw his body. The body belonged to him. He knew his body had become old and frail; he could feel it and could see it. He equally knew his wife was barren; he was very much aware of that. But he refused to consider it! That's what faith is.

Faith doesn't mean that you don't feel the pain. Faith doesn't mean that you can't see the trouble. Faith means "I see the trouble alright, but I refuse to consider it; I refuse to let it dictate the circumstances of my life or my existence. I refuse to let it dictate how I'm going to behave." You tell yourself, "I'm not going to let what I see, how I feel and everything I know that's contrary to God's Word run my life. I refuse to consider anything but God's Word!" Boy, that's strong faith!

Learn and employ this important truth: in everything, consider God's Word only! Let God's Word be the only thing that moves you. Let it be what forms your beliefs, impressions and mindset about life. Let it be the only truth, the only information by which you live. Then your life will be an unending stream of success, peace, progress and prosperity.

This is where some folks miss the mark in their faith-walk; they stagger at the promise of God – the

Word of God. One time they believe and another time, they don't believe. In a moment, they'll say "I believe God; I believe His Word." The next moment, they'll say; "Oh God please help me believe."

Don't stagger at the promise of God through unbelief. In other words, don't let unbelief run your life. The Bible says Abraham staggered not at the promise of God through unbelief, but was strong in faith, giving glory to God. He kept on testifying. He refused to stagger. As far as he was concerned, God had done it already, so he maintained his confession.

In your life, this is what you must do. God's words to you are, 'yea and amen' (2 Corinthians 1:20); that means they're settled and established. Your role is to believe them and give no place to doubt and unbelief. Be addicted to God's Word. Groom yourself to see whatever God says to you in His Word as the highest law to live by. Tell yourself, "If God said it, then it's done, for His Word never fails. Therefore I refuse to doubt; I refuse to stagger or allow doubt and unbelief choke His Word in my heart." Then you begin to glorify Him for His Word.

Maybe you woke up one day and suddenly discovered a growth somewhere in your body, and then you acted your faith and commanded the growth to disappear. From then on, do like Abraham. Even if you can still see the growth, refuse to consider it! Start giving glory to God. Keep praising Him and start telling everybody that God's Word says you were healed; therefore no growth can survive in your body. Keep testifying about it; give an offering for it. Tell everybody the growth is gone; you already have your miracle.

This was what Abraham did which was pleasing in the sight of God and made Him qualify Abraham's faith as strong faith. Abraham glorified God for His Word and told everybody his name was no longer Abram (exalted or assumed father), but Abraham, which meant 'father of many'. They must have laughed him to scorn, asking, "So, where are the children?"

But he knew he already had God's Word. Therefore, as far as he was concerned, his children were inside him. He was already 'father of many'. You know, if you're a pastor or a minister and you're reading this book, you too can become Abraham. You can begin to see your church and ministry grow with so many members inside you.

Have the doctors told you that it's impossible for you to have children because your fallopian tube is blocked or has been removed? Act on these truths that I'm sharing with you! Become Abraham! Begin to see your children inside you. Like Abraham, refuse to stagger in unbelief. Everyone will see you carry your baby before you know it. All you need do is refuse to stagger at God's Word. Set your gaze on the Word.

Become Fully Persuaded

You know, unbelief is a spirit. Fear also is a spirit and they try to attack people. When fear or unbelief attacks you, go on your knees before God; put your Bible right in front of you! Don't only read or meditate on the scriptures, but also begin to quote them out openly. Begin to say them until you're fully saturated. The Bible says, "*When the clouds are full of rain, they empty themselves,*" (Ecclesiastes 11:3); meaning there would be an overflow. That's when you become fully persuaded!

This is the third characteristics of strong faith. When your faith is strong, you're fully persuaded about God's Word. At this time, not a demon hatched out of hell will be able to convince you to doubt or stagger at God's Word. You know you have your miracle, irrespective of what the circumstances indicate. You come to that specific, unassumed knowledge that, whatever God has promised, He's faithful and able to perform. Therefore you're unperturbed; you're at peace because you know you have it made! Praise God!

Abraham was fully persuaded that what God had promised, He was also able to perform (Romans

4:21). This is strong faith; and this is the faith that works.

You know, you can't be fully persuaded when you're listening to the wrong stories from people. You can't build the faith that works when you listen to everything else but God's Word. Fear will dominate you. Men talk fear. But God talks faith! For you to build your faith to that level, where you're fully persuaded and convinced about God's Word to you, you need to keep listening to the Word. Keep getting the Word of God into your system.

Don't allow information from the newspapers, which are always laden with fear and unbelief cause you to stagger at God's Word. When you keep listening to the news on television, you'll hear a lot of words that inspire fear. But when you dominate and control your mind with the Word of God, you will become fully persuaded.

Until you're fully persuaded, you may stagger. You'll be unsure and unconvinced about God's

Word. That's when you start asking yourself "I wonder if this Word that I've been confessing for so long is really going to come to pass?"

Realize that as you keep bombarding your mind with the Word of God, you'll become fully persuaded about God's promise to the point it becomes the only thing you think and talk about. That's when doubt and unbelief become completely subdued in your life.

Jesus said,

> "For verily I say unto you, That whosoever shall say unto this mountain, Be thou removed, and be thou cast into the sea; and shall not DOUBT in his heart, but shall believe that those things which he saith shall come to pass; he shall have whatsoever he saith" (Mark 11:23).

Doubt or unbelief is the greatest thief of God's

blessings. Jesus tells us that when you don't doubt in your heart, anything you say with your mouth will come to pass. For that to happen, you must be fully and completely persuaded. You must mount a guard on your heart that says: NO DOUBT ALLOWED!

This is what you need if you've been diagnosed with cancer, HIV, diabetes or any other kind of sickness, disease or infirmity. Maybe you were told it's impossible for you to be a success in anything in life. You don't need prayer! You don't need to cry, beg or run around looking for some help from man.

Instead, begin to meditate on the Word of God. Become **FULLY** persuaded about what it says. Become fully persuaded that you're a bundle of success; you have an excellent spirit and have been ordained to prosper in all things.

Become fully persuaded that you're not the sick seeking healing! Become fully persuaded that you're a new creature; a partaker, sharer, participator in the divine nature. Therefore, sickness, disease and infirmity **CANNOT** thrive in your body – they just can't stay! Become fully persuaded of these things.

Chapter Eight

The Conquering Power Of Faith

In John 16:33, Jesus said to His disciples,

> **"These things I have spoken unto you, that in me ye might have peace. In the world ye shall have tribulation: BUT BE OF GOOD CHEER; I HAVE OVERCOME THE WORLD"**

For our faith to work, we must learn to speak

like Jesus. Every word Jesus spoke when He walked the face of the earth came to pass. Nobody ever spoke like Him. Every time He opened His mouth to speak, He spoke words of faith that produced results.

This is what the religious folks back in the days of Jesus didn't like about Him. They crucified Him because of His words, nothing else! His confessions were too powerful for the natural mind to comprehend. He confessed Himself to be the Son of God, and the religious folks hated Him for that.

When He spoke, blindness left, deaf ears were unstopped, the lame got up to walk, maimed limbs were made whole, and the dead were raised. His Words were different; they were not ordinary. Whenever He spoke, significant changes took place in the lives of His hearers. Demons cried in horror and scampered in terror.

It wasn't His touch that produced the miracles but His words. Words that were full of power. Here, in John 16:33, Jesus made a powerful confession and said to His disciples, *"Cheer up! I have overcome the world."* Nobody ever talked like Jesus! How could He say, "I have overcome the world" when He hadn't even gone to the cross, much less risen from the dead!

He said these words before He went to the Cross – before His death, burial and resurrection. Therefore, we ought to find out how He overcame the world because it's obvious He did something you and I can do.

I found out from the Bible that Jesus overcame the world by speaking faith-filled words, and discovered I can do the same thing.

Faith: The Victory That Overcomes The World!

Remember, Jesus made this world. The Bible says without Him was not anything made that was made (John 1:3). There was nothing in the system of this world that wasn't subject to Jesus. He exercised dominion over all things. He tamed them by His words – faith-filled words!

He spoke to maimed limbs, corpses, deaf ears, blind eyes, crippled limbs, demons of darkness, fishes, trees and they obeyed Him. He tamed the laws of nature and transcended them. He was never a victim. He walked on water, spoke to the wind and calmed the storm! When He encountered the leprous and said, *"Be clean!"* the leprosy disappeared.

He knew who He was! He was never afraid of anything. Everyone wondered at Him when He spoke. He didn't mince words in declaring His identity. He said I and my Father are one (John 10:30); He walked in union with the Father.

Just like Jesus, the words we speak are spirit and they are life (John 6:63). That means our words are not empty. They're potent; they have conquering, overcoming and prevailing power over devils, adversities and every negative circumstance of life.

This is why it's so important that we talk like Jesus by releasing faith-filled words.

No wonder John cried *"This is the victory that overcomes the world, even our faith"* (1 John 5:4). Our faith is the victory that overcomes the world. Our faith has supernatural power to conquer, tame and subdue the world. Hebrews 11 gives us a catalogue of faith folks - great men and women who subdued and tamed their world by faith:

> "And what shall I more say? for the time would fail me to tell of Gedeon, and of Barak, and of Samson, and of Jephthae; of David also, and Samuel, and of the prophets: Who THROUGH FAITH SUBDUED KINGDOMS, wrought righteousness, obtained promises, stopped the mouths of lions, Quenched the violence of fire, escaped the edge of the sword, out of weakness were made

> strong, waxed valiant in fight, turned
> to flight the armies of the aliens"
> (Hebrews 11:32-34).

Paul paints the picture for us of how these men subdued and conquered their world through faith. Bible history has it that John the beloved apostle, during the great persecution of the church, was covered in a cauldron of boiling oil and left to die.

But by the time all the oil burnt out, they opened it up and were shocked to see John still alive. I believe he must have pointed in their faces saying, *"Whatsoever is born of God overcomes the world!"*

Did you ever read about Samson? He tore a lion apart with his bare hands. David did the same thing. How about Daniel? He was thrown into the lion's den, and guess what he did? He didn't think about killing the lions, rather he tamed them! Then he sat with them and put his hands upon them.

I'm showing you how some of the guys from

our lineage of faith subdued their world! They dominated and conquered their world, to the point the world wasn't worthy of them anymore (Hebrews 11:38).

By their faith, they completely overcame this physical world to the point they just couldn't stay here anymore. Men like Enoch, who the Bible says *"...walked with God: and he was not; for God took him"* (Genesis 5:24). That doesn't mean God took his life or that he died, but that he walked by faith and subdued this world to the extent he was literally translated out of the world into heaven. How? By faith!

You too can do the same, and get listed in faith's hall of fame.

To know more about the ministry and messages of Pastors Chris & Anita Oyakhilome contact:

CHRIST EMBASSY

aka Believers' LoveWorld Inc.

LONDON:

Christ Embassy Int'l Office
363 Springfield Road
Chelmsford, Essex, CM2 6AW
Tel: +44 8451 240 440

SOUTH AFRICA:

303 Pretoria Avenue
Cnr. Harley and Hendrik Verwoerd,
Randburg, Gauteng
South Africa.
Tel: + 27 11 3260038; +27 72760650
+27 767805242; +27 11 8863179

NIGERIA:

P.O. Box 13563, Ikeja,
Lagos, Nigeria.
Tel: +234 - 802 3324 188,
+234 - 805 2464 131,
+234 - 1 - 892 5724

email: cec@christembassy.org
website: www.christembassy.org

Deolinda